Other books in the series:
The Crazy World of Birdwatching (Peter Rigby)
The Crazy World of Cats (Bill Stott)
The Crazy World of Gardening (Bill Stott)
The Crazy world of Golf (Mike Scott)
The Crazy World of Cricket (Bill Stott)
The Crazy World of the Handyman (Roland Fiddy)
The Crazy World of Hospitals (Bill Stott)
The Crazy World of Jogging (David Pye)
The Crazy World of Love (Roland Fiddy)
The Crazy World of Marriage (Bill Stott)
The Crazy World of Music (Bill Stott)
The Crazy World of the Office (Bill Stott)
The Crazy World of Photography (Bill Stott)
The Crazy World of Rugby (Bill Stott)
The Crazy World of the School (Bill Stott)
The Crazy World of Sex (David Pye)
The Crazy World of Skiing (Craig Peterson & Jerry Emerson)
The Crazy World of Tennis (Peter Rigby)

Published in Great Britain in 1985 by
Exley Publications Ltd, 16 Chalk Hill,
Watford, Herts WD1 4BN, United Kingdom.

Copyright © Peter Rigby, 1985
Second printing 1987
Third printing 1988
Fourth printing 1988
Fifth printing 1990
Sixth printing 1991

ISBN 1-85015-051-6

Printed and bound in Hungary.

the CRAZY world of SAILING

Cartoons by Peter Rigby

EXLEY

P.J.Rigby.

"What d'you mean, can you claim salvage? I've only just finished building her."

"Don't worry dear! The book says it always comes right after an hour or two."

"He reckons it's a newly designed rudder, so he's keeping
it under wraps!"

"It looks as if the Robinsons have been fighting again."

"*There's no need to sulk. I only said watch out for the boom, Samantha. Samantha?*"

"Just think, I might have frittered all that money away
on food and rent."

"Why on earth do you need all this self-steering gear?"

"We're half a coffee mug stain and a splash of
tomato soup away from harbour."

"Look Sir, why don't you go and get a good night's sleep. She won't be finished for weeks yet."

"I thought there would be deckchairs and Martinis."

"Now be honest. Do you think the eye-patch is overdoing it?"

"You'll be fine with me. I know these waters like the back of my hand."

"*Well, if we aren't in the shipping lane there are four moons going over at twenty knots.*"

"According to the chart, we're right in the middle of the Bermuda Triangle."

"*Excuse me. Would you happen to know if the tide's in or out?*"

"That non-slip paint must make standing a lot easier.
What d'you say?"

"I've told you before. I'm not bone-idle. I'm becalmed."

"*I only said did anyone want peanut butter on their ham sandwich.*"

"Amanda – you're on the wrong side again!"

"I know where we are all right. It's just that I don't know where any place else is!"

"O.K. then, that's agreed. I'm not cracking up. But it's still your turn to make the tea."

"You've been on that damned diet again!"

"We'll wait a bit longer. Perhaps the wind will pick up."

"*Brenda, you forgot the umbrella for keeping the pizzas dry.*"

"*I imagine you'll be glad to be back on dry land.*"

"I've had enough of this. You give him a turn on the tiller
– and you give him his cap back."

"*Speaking of the sea. Which way is it exactly?*"

"He says we certainly can't bring the dog on shore, and he's not too happy about letting you land either."

"Yes, I do know the penalty for mutiny, and no, I'm not making more coffee."

"I said 'Shove the oar in the <u>rollocks</u>'!"

"And remember – no peeking. It's to be a surprise."

"Right, that's the vital supplies. Fifty bottles and eighty cans."

"You forgot the what!!?"

"In the future would you mind calling 'land ahoy' when you see it, not when we're on it."

"Just think Muriel, if I hadn't invested in this boat you would have been getting all wrinkled up under a hot Mediterranean sun."

"It can be lonely. But then again there's the sailing season."

P.J.Rigby

"*Hope he doesn't fall in. There'd be an oil slick right across the bay.*"

"Oh, and do you have anything to remove salt-water stains?"

"I may not know much, but I know this isn't island hopping."

"There is just one thing. I presume you do play Bridge?"

"We're through the storm fellas. It'll be plain sailing from here."

"Yes I know I said we'd be in dock for lunch. Are you sure
your watch isn't fast?"

"Don't grumble. Have you any idea just how much moorings would cost in the marina?"

"Better check our bearings again. We don't want to
miss the Thames Estuary."

"I know exactly what I'm talking about. Those rocks way over there are the only hazards in these waters."

"*Get that washing in! You're signalling an obscene suggestion.*"

"Don't give me that old line, I'm not stupid. Out of wind indeed!"

"You know the type. Probably runs a vintage Bentley too."

"It's just that I imagined we'd have a lifejacket each."

"Quick, get it in the car while there's no one around."

"I see Sir. You haven't had a drink, you were just tacking into the wind."

"Yes, I remember you now. Eric Scrimshaw! We were on the same sailing course together."

"I was just saying how nice it is to see all the familiar faces each year."

"Come on, now you've seen her, you have to admit it was worth going without a few little luxuries."

"No one's even going to notice you've lost your toupee."

"Wow, what a turn! I had no <u>idea</u> you could handle a boat like this <u>B</u>elinda."

"That was your kick-o-gram. The message reads 'Happy
anniversary from your wife'."

"*Sea-Pirate to Viking Raider. Do you have a teeny-weeny drop of milk we could have?*"

"Anyone seen the latrine bucket?"

"If he says he's got salt-water in his blood once more there's going to be blood in this salt-water."

"You don't mind do you?"

"We don't have an echo sounder so Rita just pops over the side."

"I'll make a deal. I'll stop calling this the kitchen if you'll stop calling me Mr Christian."

"What's Russian for 'Sorry guys, our navigator's an idiot'?"

"I suppose you could say that the secret of off-shore sailing is to keep off the shore."

"Sorry buddy, we didn't even notice you down there."

"Come to think of it, you could be right. 'Power' does come before 'sail'."

"*You know, there is such a thing as over-confidence, Wade.*"

"Oh yes, she's a beauty. Just listen to the sound of those timbers creaking."

"It's a pleasant little marina and of course you get a much
better type of flotsam."

Books from the "Crazy World" series:

The Crazy World of Birdwatching. £3.99. By Peter Rigby. Over seventy cartoons on the strange antics of the twitcher brigade. One of our most popular pastimes, this will be a natural gift for any birdwatcher.

The Crazy World of Cats. £3.99. By Bill Stott. Fat cats, alley cats, lazy cats, sneaky cats – from the common moggie to the pedigree Persian – you'll find them all in this witty collection. If you've ever wondered what your cat was really up to, this is for you.

The Crazy World of Cricket. £3.99. By Bill Stott. This must be Bill Stott's silliest cartoon collection. It makes an affectionate present for any cricketer who can laugh at himself.

The Crazy World of Gardening. £3.99. By Bill Stott. The perfect present for anyone who has ever wrestled with a lawnmower that won't start, over-watered a pot plant or been assaulted by a rose bush from behind.

The Crazy World of Golf. £3.99. By Mike Scott. Over seventy hilarious cartoons show the frantic golfer in his (or her) every absurdity. What really goes on out on the course, and the golfer's life when not playing are chronicled in loving detail.

The Crazy World of the Handyman. £3.99. By Roland Fiddy. This book is a must for anyone who has ever hung *one* length of wallpaper upside down or drilled through an electric cable. A gift for anyone who has ever tried to "do it yourself" and failed!

The Crazy World of Hospitals. £3.99. By Bill Stott. Hilarious cartoons about life in a hospital. A perfect present for a doctor or a nurse – or a patient who needs a bit of fun.

The Crazy World of Love. £3.99. By Roland Fiddy. This funny yet tender collection covers every aspect of love from its first joys to its dying embers. An ideal gift for lovers of all ages to share with each other.

The Crazy World of Marriage. £3.99. By Bill Stott. The battle of the sexes in close-up from the altar to the grave, in public and in private, in and out of bed. See your friends, your enemies (and possibly yourselves?) as never before!

The Crazy World of Music. £3.99. By Bill Stott. This upbeat collection will delight music-lovers of all ages. From Beethoven to Wagner and from star conductor to the humblest orchestra member, no-one escapes Bill Stott's penetrating pen.

The Crazy World of the Office. £3.99. By Bill Stott. Laugh your way through the office jungle with Bill Stott as he observes the idiosyncrasies of bosses, the deviousness of underlings and the goings-on at the Christmas party. . . . A must for anyone who has ever worked in an office.

The Crazy World of Photography. £3.99. By Bill Stott. Everyone who owns a camera, be it a Box Brownie or the latest Pentax, will find something to laugh at in this superb collection. The absurdities of the camera freak will delight your whole family.

The Crazy World of Rugby. £3.99. By Bill Stott. From schoolboy to top international player, no-one who plays or watches rugby will escape Bill Stott's merciless expose of their habits and absurdities. Over seventy hilarious cartoons – a must for addicts.

The Crazy World of the School. £3.99. By Bill Stott. A brilliant and hilarious reminder of those chalk throwing days. Wince at Bill Stott's wickedly funny new collection of crazy school capers.

The Crazy World of Sex. £3.99. By David Pye. A light-hearted look at the absurdities and weaker moments of human passion – the turn-ons and the turn-offs. Very funny and in (reasonably) good taste.

The Crazy World of Skiing. £3.99. By Craig Peterson and Jerry Emerson. Covering almost every possible (and impossible) experience on the slopes, this is an ideal present for anyone who has ever strapped on skis – and instantly fallen over.

The Crazy World of Tennis. £3.99. By Peter Rigby. Would-be Stephen Edbergs and Steffi Grafs watch out! This brilliant collection will pin-point their pretensions and poses. Whether you play by yourself or only watch TV, this will amuse and entertain you!

These books make super presents. Order them from your local bookseller or from Exley Publications Ltd, Dept BP, 16 Chalk Hill, Watford, Herts WD1 4BN. (Please send £1.50 for one book or £2.25 for two or more to cover postage and packing.)